GREG LAURIE

HOPE FOR AMERICA

KERYGMA
PUBLISHING

ALLEN
DAVID
BOOKS

©2012 by Greg Laurie. All rights reserved.

International Standard Book Number: 978-1-61291-349-0

Published by Kerygma Publishing

Cover design by Mattson Creative

Coordination: FM Management, Ltd.

Contact: mark@fmmgt.net

Unless otherwise indicated, all Scripture quotations are taken from: *The Holy Bible*, New King James Version © 1984 by Thomas Nelson, Inc.

Scripture quotations marked (NIV) are from *The Holy Bible*, New International Version®. Copyright © 1973, 1978, 1984 by Biblica. Used by permission of Zondervan Publishing House.

Scripture quotations marked (NLT) are taken from The New Living Translation, copyright © 1996, 2004, 2007 by Tyndale House Foundation. Used by permission of Tyndale House Publishers Inc., Carol Stream, Illinois 60188. All rights reserved.

Scripture quotations marked (TLB) are taken from The Living Bible, copyright © 1971 by Tyndale House Publishers, Wheaton, Illinois.

Scripture quotations marked (MSG) are taken from The Message, by Eugene Peterson. 1993, 1994, 1995, 1996, 2000, 2001, 2002. Used by permission of NavPress Publishing Group. All rights reserved.

Scripture quotations marked (PH) are from The New Testament in Modern English, Revised Edition © 1958, 1960, 1972 by J. B. Phillips.

Scripture quotations marked (KJV) are taken from *The Holy Bible,* King James Version. Public domain.

Printed in the United States of America

1 2 3 4 5 6 7 8 / 17 16 15 14 13 12

CHAPTER 1

Through my years of ministry, I have had the opportunity to travel around the world and visit many countries. Some have been truly great nations I would be happy to visit again. Other nations have been places I would go back to if the Lord called me there but I'd just as soon leave off my itinerary. Through it all, I have become more convinced than ever that the United States of America is still the greatest country on the face of the earth. I have always believed that, and I still believe that—in spite of our problems, and in spite of the fact that many in our nation have turned away from the God of our fathers.

As I write these words, our country is in the midst of yet another political cycle, with a number of people running for the presidency. Every night on the news or in the course of political debates, we hear this person or that person give his or her views on what has gone wrong in our country and how that individual would fix it.

There is certainly a place for Christians in politics, and it's a benefit to everyone to have godly men and women in public office. I believe that it's an important responsibility of every Christian American to register and vote.

Nevertheless, we need to remember this: Politics are not the ultimate solution to our country's needs. I believe the only real and lasting solution for the United States of America is for us to turn back to God. Frankly, I don't see any other hope. I think America has two options before us right now: judgment or revival.

A CHRISTIAN FOUNDATION UNDER ATTACK

Those who seek to rewrite history now claim that America was never founded on Judeo-Christian principles. They have a lot of work to do because the preponderance of evidence leads honest scholars and observers in the opposite direction.

If you take time to read the statements from our nation's founders, as well as the founders of many of our great universities and places of learning, there is no denying the fact that America was built on a godly foundation. Consider just one piece of evidence. What follows is an excerpt from the very first prayer uttered in the halls of Congress:

O Lord our Heavenly Father, high and mighty King of kings, and Lord of lords, who dost from thy throne behold all the dwellers on earth and reignest with power supreme and uncontrolled over all the Kingdoms, Empires and Governments; look down in mercy, we beseech Thee, on these our American States, who have fled to Thee from the rod of the oppressor and thrown themselves on Thy gracious protection, desiring to be henceforth dependent only on Thee. . . .

Be Thou present, O God of wisdom, and direct the councils of this honorable assembly; enable them to settle things on the best and surest foundation. . . .

Shower down on them and the millions they here represent, such temporal blessings as Thou seest expedient for them in this world and crown them with everlasting glory in the world to come. All this we ask

in the name and through the merits of Jesus Christ,
Thy Son and our Savior.

Amen.[1]

I wonder what would happen if that prayer were
prayed today in Congress. In the twenty-first century,
we have an atheist group in federal court, suing over the
fact that the name of Jesus Christ was invoked in our
current president's inauguration ceremony. Things have
certainly changed a great deal since our founding.

No, not all of our founding fathers were Christians,
though many of them were. Most at least had a respect
for the Word of God and believed it to be an authorita-
tive source. And they believed in the person and the
power of Jesus Christ.

George Washington, our first president, stated,
"To the distinguished Character of Patriot, it should be
our highest Glory to add the more distinguished
Character of Christian."

Thomas Jefferson, our third president, wrote, "Can
the liberties of a nation be thought secure when we have
removed their only firm basis, a conviction in the minds
of the people that these liberties are a gift from God.

. . . Indeed, I tremble for my country when I reflect that God is just; that His justice cannot sleep forever."[2]

Patrick Henry, one of those who ratified our country's constitution, wrote, "It cannot be emphasized too strongly or too often that this great Nation was founded not by religionists but by Christians, not on religions but on the gospel of Jesus Christ. For this reason alone, people of other faiths have been afforded freedom of worship here."[3]

If we remove that foundation, if we remove that belief in the Bible as the Word of God, we're left with a vacuum and suddenly this whole American experiment begins to collapse like a house of cards.

What our founders gave us was freedom *of* religion, not freedom *from* religion. And they led the way with a strong belief in and respect for the authority of the Word of God.

When our public school system was founded, the two books you could find in every classroom were a copy of the Bible and *The Pilgrim's Progress*, the classic Christian allegory written by John Bunyan. Our great universities, such as Harvard and Princeton, were originally established as Christian institutions. Within

Harvard's original rules and precepts, it was written that everyone shall "consider well the main end of his life and studies is to know God and Jesus Christ which is eternal life."[4]

Can you see how far we have fallen away from these founding principles as a culture? You won't find the Bible in public-school classrooms today. When I was growing up, I remember the Ten Commandments being posted on the wall of our classroom. Sadly, those days are long gone. Teachers can no longer open class with a word of prayer as they once did, and now even a moment of silence is unacceptable.

Our public officials and courts have done their very best to take God out of the classroom and out of contemporary culture. People laugh at the Christian worldview today. As a result, even matters of simple common sense have been turned on their heads. Up is down. Bad is good. Right is wrong. Wrong is right. Dark is light.

I believe that many of America's problems started back in the 1960s, when I was growing up. The liberal social experimentation of that decade has turned into an epidemic in the twenty-first century. Sociologist Robert Nisbet wrote, "The ideologies which gained entry into the academy in the sixties claimed that the fundamental intellectual principles of Western culture were illegitimate and must be overthrown. With that destroyed terms like truth, good, evil, and soul could be discarded."

So that's where we are today.

In our institutions of learning—public schools and colleges—evolution is taught as fact, even though it is disputed in the scientific community. And no consideration will be given to teaching creationism or even intelligent design as viable alternatives. In fact, it isn't even an option.

As a result, our children are instructed from their earliest science classes that life on earth began in a pool of ooze and that they are highly evolved animals, with apes and monkeys for ancestors. There is no right or wrong. There is no God. There will be no final judgment or accountability for our actions. And then we scratch our heads and wonder why a kid would walk onto a high school campus and start randomly shooting people.

It's almost bewildering—if it weren't so tragic—to hear television pundits saying, "Why would this happen?"

But why wouldn't it happen?

If there is no God, no heaven and hell, no right and wrong or good or evil, why would we expect people to live morally?

That is why our only hope as a nation is to not merely return to conservative values but also return to the biblical truth we find in the pages of Scripture.

"WE HAVE FORGOTTEN GOD"

Our problem in America has been identified by President Abraham Lincoln, who more than a century ago wrote these words: "We have forgotten God. We have forgotten the gracious Hand which preserved us in peace, and multiplied and enriched and strengthened us; and we have vainly imagined, in the deceitfulness of our hearts, that all these blessings were produced by some superior wisdom and virtue of our own."[5]

President Lincoln was right. We have forgotten God.

But here is the good news: God has not forgotten us.

Still, we look at everything happening in our nation and ask ourselves, "Will it ever get better?" At the beginning of the millennium, in the year 2000, there was a buoyant optimism among Americans about the future. At that time, 28 percent of Americans said they were dissatisfied with the way things were in our country, and 69 percent were very satisfied.

Now, fast-forward to today. A recent poll reveals that 90 percent of Americans are dissatisfied with our situation. The *Wall Street Journal* did a poll that revealed that 73 percent of Americans believe that the United States is in a state of decline.

What interests me is that polls seem to reveal an amazing contradiction in our country. According to recent surveys, 94 percent of Americans believe in God, 84 percent believe that Jesus is God, 66 percent say they have made a personal commitment to Jesus Christ, and 31 percent describe themselves as "born again." And more than three quarters of the population believes that the Bible is the Word of God.

Really?

Those stats sound pretty good, right?

So what is going on with our culture? Another poll revealed that 69 percent of Americans believe there is no such thing as absolute truth. How does that work?

How could almost 70 percent of Americans say there is no such thing as absolute truth, while almost the same amount say they believe the Bible is the Word of God? What's going on here?

THE COLLAPSE OF THE FAMILY

I believe that many of our nation's social ills can be traced directly to the breakdown of the American family. There was a day, not so very long ago, when children being born out of wedlock were the exception, not the rule. I read a recent statistic that said more children are now born out of wedlock than are born into a family with a husband and wife.

As a result, the whole concept of an American family is being challenged and redefined. Our news and entertainment media keep repeating the same lies over and over again, saying that a man and a woman living together is the same as being married or that a homosexual relationship is the same as a man and a woman together.

This radical social experiment we are engaging in as a country today is already producing more troubles than we can begin to deal with. Most studies reveal that the problems that develop in a young person's life can be traced back to a broken family and specifically to the absence of a father.

Check out these statistics: 63 percent of youth suicides are committed by children from fatherless homes; 95 percent of all homeless and runaway children are from fatherless homes; 71 percent of high school dropouts are from fatherless homes; 85 percent of all youths sitting in prison today are from fatherless homes. And it all results from the breakdown of the family as God has established it.

It has been said that a family can survive without a nation but a nation cannot survive without the family. So, as the Bible clearly tells us, we have sown the wind and are now reaping the whirlwind (see Hosea 8:7).

That leaves us with two options as a nation: judgment or revival.

WHAT IS "REVIVAL"?

We throw around the word *revival*, but what do we mean by it?

Some might envision a bunch of people crammed into a church, yelling and screaming, hot and sweating, with maybe a few snakes being passed around. For others, a revival might simply be a sign or reader board down at the local church on the corner that says, "Revival meetings, this week only, 7:00 p.m. to 9:00 p.m."

The fact is, these may be outstanding meetings, and people can call them "revival meetings" if they want to. But they do not represent true revival, in the classic sense of the term.

So what do we mean when we say we need a revival? C. H. Spurgeon defined revival as "to live again, to receive again a life which has almost expired; to rekindle into a flame the vital spark which was nearly extinguished."[6]

A revival, then, means to come back to life.

Another said, "Revival is a time when heaven draws closer to earth." Revival is for the church. When we speak of a revival, what we are really saying is that God's people need to get back to living the Christian life as it was meant to be lived. And if Christians across America are truly "revived," they will have an impact on our country and its future direction.

REVIVAL BEGINS WITH YOU

Revival is for only the believer. As Spurgeon said, "To be revived is a blessing which can only be enjoyed by those who have some degree of life. Those who have no spiritual life are not, and cannot be, in the strictest sense of the term, subjects of revival."[7] A true revival is to be looked for in the church of God.

One person defined revival as "a beginning of new obedience to God." It begins when each of us takes an honest look at ourselves and asks questions such as, *How am I doing right now spiritually? Was there a time when my faith was stronger than it is today? Was there a time I loved the Word of God—reading it, memorizing it, thinking about it, and hearing it taught—more than I do today?*

How about prayer? Maybe prayer was something you loved to do. You found yourself talking to God throughout the day and maybe even waking up in the middle of the night thinking about Him, speaking to Him, and listening for His voice. Prayer was second nature to you, like breathing. Is it still that way today?

How about being a part of the church? Maybe you can look back on a time when you loved getting up on

Sunday mornings and being in church with God's people. Maybe you used to attend a midweek study or a Bible study in someone's home and you just couldn't get enough of it.

Is it still like that for you? Could it be that you need revival? It may be that you need to "come back to life" and allow the Lord to kindle a fresh fire in your spirit.

Martyn Lloyd-Jones defined revival this way: "Revival awakens in our hearts an increased awareness of the presence of God, a new love for God, new hatred for sin, and a hunger for His Word." Does that describe you right now? Do you have a hatred for sin and a hunger for His Word?

Some might say, "Greg, I'm actually happy the way I am. I don't think that America needs revival, and I don't think I need it either." That is totally your choice. You don't have to be revived if you don't want to be. Leonard Ravenhill said, "As long as we are content to live without revival, we will." Nevertheless, the heart cry of every child of God ought to be for the Lord to send an awakening to our nation.

Habakkuk 3:2 says,

Lᴏʀᴅ, I have heard of your fame;

> I stand in awe of your deeds, O Lᴏʀᴅ.

Renew them in our day,

> in our time make them known;
>
> in wrath remember mercy. (ɴɪᴠ)

The prophet was saying, "Lord, we want to see it again. We want to see Your strong hand at work around us. We've heard about the good old days and all those great awakenings of the past, but we want to see it in our day, Lord. Revive Your work."

Have you ever prayed a prayer like that? Psalm 85:6 says, "Will You not revive us again, that Your people may rejoice in You?" Another translation says, "Why not help us make a fresh start—a resurrection life? Then your people will laugh and sing!" (ᴍsɢ).

As I said, the United States has two options: judgment or revival.

WHERE IS AMERICA IN PROPHECY?

Here is what concerns me. As I study the Scriptures and Bible prophecy of the end times, I can't find the

United States. Here we are, the undisputed superpower of the whole planet, and there isn't so much as a word about our future or how we fit into end-times events. We can find smaller nations, such as Iran and of course Israel. Some say that China and Russia are identifiable in Scripture. But where are the passages that clearly speak of America?

There really is no definitive word in Scripture about the United States in the last days. One thing seems clear: We won't have the standing in the world that we have today—not even close. I'm not saying that America won't exist as the end times players play their parts; I'm just saying that it will be a very different America from the one we know right now.

So why is this? Let's consider some possibilities.

1. America could be devastated by a nuclear war.

As horrific a scenario as this might be, you simply can't dismiss it out of hand. We've had adversaries such as Russia and China for many years, but now we have rogue nations such as North Korea developing nuclear weapons. Iran is believed to be developing nuclear capability and has repeatedly threatened to wipe the nation of Israel off the map. They have threatened to use such weapons against the United States as well. What's more, there are nuclear weapons unaccounted for since the breakup of the Soviet Union. If one or more of those weapons ended up in the hands of a terrorist group and were detonated in an American city, it would make 9/11 pale in comparison.

So we can't say it would never happen. It could happen. Let's pray that it never will.

2. We could drastically decline as a world power.

Some say we're already on the road to this end. If America continues much further along the path we are already on, systematically eliminating God and His Word from our culture, our schools, and the public square, we simply could collapse as a world power and as an economic power in our world.

We know this much: The Bible teaches that a new superpower will emerge in the last days. He is identified as the Antichrist and will have ten nations confederated behind him. It could be that the United States will be so marginalized as a world power that we simply will fall in line with the other nations behind the Antichrist.

Those are both realistic (if unpleasant) scenarios for our country. But I have a third one that I greatly prefer.

3. We could experience a massive spiritual awakening that spreads across our country, and millions in our population would be swept up in the Rapture.

That is certainly a scenario that would explain why our nation isn't mentioned in prophecy. Many of us might be caught up in the air with Jesus when He comes for His church.

Let's just pull a number out of the air and say there are fifty million born-again Christians in America. Do you think it would affect our country if—in a moment, in the twinkling of an eye—fifty million people vanished? Think of it! These would include people in industry, government, the military, business, agriculture, finance, education, medicine, and law enforcement. These would be people running hospitals, banks, schools, communications networks, and the power grid. What if that many of America's citizens suddenly disappeared? Can you see why America might not be a player in the final last-days drama?

So here is the question: Is there a historical

precedent for a nation heading in the wrong direction to turn around and go the right direction and have her life extended?

The answer is yes, and I could give many examples. But for the remaining pages of this chapter, I want to offer one dramatic biblical example.

AN EVIL EMPIRE FACES JUDGMENT

Nineveh was the capital of the mighty Assyrian empire, which was the superpower of her day. It took three days to circle metropolitan Nineveh. Her population was around one million, similar in size to San Francisco.

The Assyrian capital was a heavily fortified city encompassed by five walls and three moats. The major wall was fifty feet high, extended for eight miles, and was wide enough for four chariots to ride abreast on the top.

Ninevites lived large. They enjoyed the best chariots, the finest food, and the most exotic entertainment. They boasted an extensive business and commercial system like the world had never seen, and Assyria had enjoyed its status as a superpower for some two hundred years.

At the time the book of Jonah was written, Assyria had the most powerful military anywhere (although the power of Babylon was growing in the southeast). She was the undisputed superpower.

Nineveh's days, however, were numbered. Why? Because she was wicked—wicked enough to appear on God's radar, so to speak. In Jonah 1:2, the Bible tells us that the wickedness of Nineveh had come up before God. Another way to translate that would be to say that their evil reached a high degree, or the highest pitch.

Have you ever missed taking your trash out for a week or two? The garbage is almost overflowing and—especially if the weather has been hot—it smells *really* bad. That is how Nineveh was. It was like a moral trash heap that was stinking to high heaven. This was a military power renowned for its violence and sadistic cruelty. It wasn't enough for the Ninevites to simply sweep in and conquer a city; they would torture and murder the nation's inhabitants in cold blood and take great delight in doing so. Historical records tell us that the Ninevites would take the boys and girls of a conquered people and burn them alive. They would torture adults by literally tearing the skin from their bodies and leaving them to die in the scorching sun. And they *celebrated* such things.

Finally, God said, in essence, "This stinks, and I'm going to judge this place." But because of God's being who He is, He wanted to give the Ninevites one last chance to change their minds, turn from their sins, and repent. That's when the Lord called His prophet Jonah and told him to go to the Ninevites and preach to them. That would be like God saying to a patriotic Israeli today, "Go and preach to Iran because I want to spare them." The Israeli might say, "Are You kidding me? I don't *want* to spare Iran. Iran threatens every day to wipe us off the face of the earth. Why don't You just go ahead and take care of them? You would be doing us all a favor!"

Jonah hated the Ninevites with everything in him. He wanted them to be judged, he wanted them to be wiped out, and he *didn't* want to preach to them and give them a chance to be saved. So Jonah the prophet flatly refused the Lord's command, went down to the harbor, and caught a ship heading away from Nineveh.

We can all come down on Jonah and say how

wrong he was to be so close-minded in refusing to preach to the Ninevites. But hasn't God called us all to preach the gospel? How are you doing on that? When was the last time you engaged someone with the gospel message? We have all fallen short when it comes to preaching the gospel.

How about taking the gospel to an enemy? Probably not. Most of us don't even want to take the gospel to our friends, much less people who hate us or oppose us.

Why didn't Jonah want to do this? Because he knew God. He knew that the God he served was a loving, forgiving God, and the last thing he wanted was for the Ninevites to be loved and forgiven.

Sometimes you will hear people say, "I believe in the God of the New Testament, but I don't believe in the God of the Old Testament because He is angry and wrathful."

May I be blunt? That is such a stupid statement.

The God of the Old Testament is the same as the God of the New Testament. And the so-called "God of the Old Testament" is described by Jonah, the Lord's prophet, in these terms:

This is exactly what I thought you'd do, Lord, when I was there in my own country and you first told me to come here. That's why I ran away to Tarshish. *For I knew you were a gracious God, merciful, slow to get angry, and full of kindness; I knew how easily you could cancel your plans for destroying these people.* (Jonah 4:2, TLB, emphasis added)

And so it was that Jonah, in an effort to ditch this assignment from God, tried to run away from Him, boarding a ship bound for distant Tarshish.

NINEVEH (AND JONAH) GET A SECOND CHANCE

No sooner did the runaway prophet's ship get out to sea, however, when the Lord sent a monster storm so that the sailors on board despaired of life. The crew of that distressed vessel finally determined that Jonah, an Israelite, was the one responsible for their peril and that he had been running away from God. Eventually, Jonah directed them to throw him overboard so that God would relent and the storm would leave them in peace.

That's just what those sailors did. They tossed

Jonah into the angry sea, and everyone on board (and Jonah) thought that was the end of him. But the Bible tells us that the Lord had prepared a great fish to swallow Jonah, and the prophet ended up in that fish's gullet for three days and three nights. (This was like sushi eating in reverse; instead of man eating fish, this was fish eating man.)

And in that terrible place, with his head wrapped in seaweed, the prophet had a little prayer meeting and changed his mind about going to Nineveh. God commanded the fish to vomit Jonah onto dry land, and as the waterlogged prophet was sitting there on the beach, trying to get his bearings and the seaweed out of his ears, God spoke to Him again. To me, it's one of the most hopeful passages in the whole Bible:

> Now the word of the LORD came to Jonah *the second time*, saying, "Arise, go to Nineveh, that great city, and preach to it the message that I tell you." (Jonah 3:1-2, emphasis added)

God was giving His servant a second chance to get it right. Where would I be—where would any of us be — if we didn't serve a God who gave second chances? And third chances? And seven hundredth chances?

So it was Nineveh or bust. Jonah, the original chicken of the sea, set off to do what God already had told him to do.

We pick up the story again in verses 3-4:

> Jonah arose and went to Nineveh, according to the word of the LORD. Now Nineveh was an exceedingly great city, a three-day journey in extent. And Jonah began to enter the city on the first day's walk. Then he cried out and said, "Yet forty days, and Nineveh shall be overthrown!"

There was no promise of forgiveness. It was strictly a message of judgment and doom: "You're all going to die!" There was no invitation to repent and come forward for counseling, and there was no choir singing "Just As I Am." But look what happened:

> The people of Nineveh believed God, proclaimed a fast, and put on sackcloth, from the greatest to the least of them. Then word came to the king of Nineveh; and he

arose from his throne and laid aside his robe, covered himself with sackcloth and sat in ashes. And he caused it to be proclaimed and published throughout Nineveh by the decree of the king and his nobles, saying,

"Let neither man nor beast, herd nor flock, taste anything; do not let them eat, or drink water. But let man and beast be covered with sackcloth, and cry mightily to God; yes, let every one turn from his evil way and from the violence that is in his hands. Who can tell if God will turn and relent, and turn away from His fierce anger, so that we may not perish?" (verses 5-9)

The whole city believed God! How serious were they about repenting? They even made their animals wear sackcloth! From the king on down, they turned from their wicked ways and turned to God with all their hearts. And what was the result? God heard their prayer, spared them, and sent a nationwide revival. Verse 10 says, "Then God saw their works, that they turned from their evil way; and God relented from the disaster that He had said He would bring upon them, and He did not do it."

It is amazing to me that the Ninevites would turn

to God after a sermon like that. There was no offer of hope and no promise of forgiveness; it was just a bare warning that judgment was on its way. And the people melted like butter before this word of the Lord.

This tells me that if God could bring a mighty revival in Nineveh, with no better representative than Jonah and no more gospel than he preached in their streets, He surely can do the same thing for America.

In the Gospels, Jesus used the story of Jonah to make a very important point:

Some of the scribes and Pharisees answered, saying, "Teacher, we want to see a sign from You."

But He answered and said to them, "An evil and adulterous generation seeks after a sign, and no sign will be given to it except the sign of the prophet Jonah. For as Jonah was three days and three nights in the belly of the great fish, so will the Son of Man be three days and three nights in the heart of the earth." (Matthew 12:38-40)

The Pharisees were saying, "Hey, do a miracle. Impress us. Entertain us." And Jesus said, in effect,

"Here's your miracle: Just as Jonah was in the belly of that fish, so I will be in the heart of the earth." In other words, He would die on a cross for the sins of the world and rise from the dead three days later.

And that is our message to take to a lost world.

Sometimes we might think that if we could perform some amazing miracle, all of our friends would believe. Would they? I don't think so. I think the most impressive thing you and I can do is live a godly life, and the most impressive thing we can say is that Jesus Christ is the way to come into a relationship with God. That is our message, and we have been commissioned to take it into all the world.

Revival has been defined as God's finger pointed at you. Do you need revival? Are you in the place you need to be in as a follower of Jesus Christ? Do you need to repent?

Revival starts with us.

Revival starts with you.

CHAPTER 2

What will be the future of the United States of America? Are we doomed to slip into mediocrity and obscurity, as with so many other nations throughout history? Will we be conquered, either militarily or economically, by a more powerful foe? Will America end up in the ash heap of history? Or are our greatest days still ahead?

No one can say with any certainty what the future of America will be, but it's worth noting that our country is not to be found in the biblical accounts of the last days. I'm not saying we won't be there in some way, shape, or form. But there is no clear passage of Scripture that even remotely identifies a major world superpower as the United States is in the world today, so it makes us wonder. Where are we, and what will happen to us? The greatest nation on earth is conspicuously absent from the world stage during the end times.

We know this much: America, like every other nation, has its days numbered. No country lasts forever. Rome was once the reigning superpower on the face of the earth, with the most powerful military the world had ever seen. Rome was eventually conquered, but before she collapsed externally, she collapsed internally.

I think we would do well to look at the soul of our country right now. Many Americans support a strong and vigorous military and believe we should be able to defend ourselves against any external threats. But what about the internal threats? What about the danger of an internal collapse?

In his excellent book *Caesar and Christ*, historian Will Durant made this observation about the fall of Rome: "A great civilization is not conquered from without until it has destroyed itself within. The essential causes of Rome's decline lay in her people, her morals, her class struggle, her failing trade, her bureaucratic despotism, her stifling taxes, her consuming wars."[1]

The United States has strayed dramatically from the original vision of our founding fathers, the men who laid the foundation for this wonderful concept we call America. We have succeeded in removing God and His Word from our schools, our sporting events, our workplaces, and the public square.

Christmas, which was once at least to some degree a celebration of the birth of Jesus, has now turned into "the holidays," "the season," or just winter solstice. Good Friday and Easter, which is a time to remember the death and resurrection of the Lord Jesus, have now become spring break. It's as though we are actively pushing against the very values upon which our nation was founded.

But here is what we need to remember: The freedom we enjoy is built on the foundation of absolute truth. And when you remove that foundation, this freedom we currently enjoy can quickly devolve into anarchy. Many in our country today invest their talents, resources, and life energies in uprooting and tearing down the moral standards that have guided our conduct for multiple generations. We don't like the idea of a family—of a man and a woman being married for life. We want the concept of "right" and "wrong" to be replaced with vague moral relativism, where we can all choose our own truths.

It reminds me of a fish I once had named Oscar.

ESCAPE TO NOWHERE

Actually, Oscar truly was an oscar.

It's a species of fish, called oscar fish. When I was growing up, I collected tropical fish. Don't ask me why. While other kids were out playing baseball, I was busy adding to my fish collection. I would get on my bicycle, ride two cities away, and bring my new acquisitions home from the pet store in little plastic bags, adding them to my tank when I got home.

I loved fish, and I was excited to bring home my first oscar fish, which I promptly named Oscar. I quickly found out something about oscars: They are very aggressive. Even when they are little, if you introduce them into an aquarium of larger fish, it won't be long until the oscar is boss of the tank, running the whole place and chasing the other fish around all day. Oscar seemed to thrive in his new world and got bigger and bigger.

One day I came home from school to check on

him in the tank, and he was gone! I looked around the tank, behind the tank. Where does a fish go? Then I looked in an open drawer right beneath the tank that had spilled birdseed in it. (I also had a parakeet named Popcorn, but that's another story.) There was Oscar, lying there in the drawer, covered in birdseed. So pitiful! He looked as though he were breaded and ready to fry; all I needed was tartar sauce. But wait . . . his gills were still moving! When I grabbed him, he started jerking around. As quickly as I could, I put some water in the bathtub and dumped him in. He immediately started swimming around, presumably blowing the birdseed out of his gills and looking for new worlds to conquer.

So Oscar lived to tell the story of his adventure and was restored to his tank. But he hadn't learned his lesson. He still jumped out a couple more times, as I recall.

What a stupid fish!

Oscar had said, "This tank is too confining. I want out of this place. I want to check out the world on the other side of the glass." So he made the leap, but it didn't work out so well for him. His gills weren't working in the open air, and I can't imagine that he was enjoying the birdseed. It turned out that he needed intervention from his owner, who actually cared about him and knew what was best for him.

America needs that kind of intervention. We need God's help, and we need it very soon.

"WE NEED GOD'S HELP"

Do you remember how many Americans turned back to God after the horrific tragedies of 9/11? Do you remember the prayer vigils on street corners? Do you recall the members of Congress spontaneously breaking into "God Bless America" on the steps of the U. S. Capitol building? Do you remember how churches were packed to capacity in the aftermath of that savage attack on our country?

People were saying, "What do we do? Where do we turn? We don't know what's happening here. We need God's help."

The urgency of that realization has faded since those days back in 2001, but the truth remains: We *do* need God's intervention, and we need it right away. If we do not experience revival as a nation and experience it soon, I believe that judgment is inevitable. Peter Marshall, the former chaplain of the U.S. Senate, made this statement: "The choice before us is plain: Christ or chaos, conviction or compromise, discipline or disintegration."[2]

In the previous chapter, we saw how God turned the evil empire of Assyria and its capital Nineveh around. It had been one of the most wicked, violent nations on the planet, infamous for its cruelty. Yet despite the fact of a rather pathetic message from Jonah, the reluctant preacher, they turned to the Lord en masse and repented of their sin.

The result?

God spared them as a nation and extended their days.

Could the Lord do that for America? I believe He could. Whether He does or not depends on us. Is there historical precedent for this? Have we ever had a sweeping revival in this country before? Yes, we have. In fact, we have had a number of them.

GREAT AWAKENINGS

The first Great Awakening happened in the 1700s, before the Revolutionary War, and was led by such men as Jonathan Edwards and George Whitefield. During just two years of this revival—from 1740 to 1742—some 25,000 to 50,000 people came to Christ. That may not seem like an impressive number, until you consider the fact that the population of our whole country at that time was only about 300,000.

The second Great Awakening, led by men such as Charles Finney, began in the 1790s and lasted until 1840. This was a time when the Wild West was beginning to open up, the law was disregarded, and sexual sin was rampant. The revivalists of that day started having what came to be known as "camp meetings." (Have you ever heard of the sawdust trail?) They would set up camps with large tents out in the middle of the woods, and they would hold meetings that were attended by thousands of people. They didn't have modern communication, and no one was updating their Facebook page or sending out Tweets about where the meetings were, yet thousands of Americans of all ages attended these meetings, and many came to faith.

The third Great Awakening was from 1857 to 1859. It began with a layman named Jeremiah Lanphier, a forty-eight-year-old businessman who lived in New York City on Fulton Street.

Lanphier had deep concerns for his city and country, so he started a little prayer meeting in the city. Initially, it was attended by only a handful, but then the stock market crashed, and soon his meeting was overflowing with praying New Yorkers. Not long after that, the city was filled with people praying every day at lunchtime in multiple locations. It wasn't long before the theaters on Broadway were filled with Christians praying for the city and the nation. Within six months, ten thousand people were gathering daily for prayer in New York City.

Can you imagine such a thing? It is reported that fifty thousand New Yorkers were converted from March to May. And during that single year, the number of reported conversions through the country reached an average of fifty thousand per week for a couple of years. When it was all said and done, nearly one million people came to faith, and it had all begun with

Jeremiah Lanphier and his little prayer meeting on Fulton Street. Lanphier wasn't a preacher or a missionary; he was just a Christian businessman who worked in an office. But when he began praying, God chose to answer those prayers in a dramatic way.

THE JESUS MOVEMENT

Remember the Jesus Movement of the late 1960s and 1970s? This was a genuine revival in our nation that many of us remember or even participated in.

During the 1960s, our nation was in great turmoil. Some may look back on those days through rose-colored granny glasses and think of that era as "the good old days." How quickly we forget! They were years marked by great uncertainty, upheaval, and fear. When I was growing up, bomb drills were mandatory in school classrooms. I remember getting under the desk and crouching down. This is what we were to do in case of an atomic war. (That would have really helped a lot, right?)

Our national innocence was shattered when we saw our young president, John F. Kennedy, shot in Dallas.

This was followed by the assassinations of Martin Luther King Jr. and Robert Kennedy, the president's brother.

The Vietnam War was raging, and young men were coming back every day in body bags. Feminists raised their voices in the workplace and on college campuses, demanding equal rights. Anti-war protests and riots disrupted the peace of many American cities, and anarchy and chaos seemed to be breaking out on all sides. As the drug culture surged among young people, the slogan of the day was "Turn on, tune in, drop out." It was all about drugs, sex, and rock 'n' roll.

By and large, the church was ill-prepared to reach the youth culture of those days. Old methods, old music, and old formulas just weren't cutting it, and the church didn't know what to do. On April 8, 1966, the cover of *Time* magazine featured big red letters on a black background, asking, "Is God dead?" And many liberal Protestant theologians said that indeed He was.

Enter the Jesus Movement.

It was divine intervention that saved a generation. A little more than five years after the "Is God Dead?" cover, the June 21, 1971, issue of *Time* featured a picture of Jesus, with the words "The Jesus Revolution."

The lead article of that issue began with these words, quoting from a poster in a popular Christian underground newspaper:

WANTED: JESUS CHRIST
ALIAS: THE MESSIAH, THE SON OF GOD, KING OF
    KINGS, LORD OF LORDS, PRINCE OF PEACE, ETC.
> Notorious leader of an underground liberation
    movement . . .

And the *Time* magazine quote ended with these words:

BEWARE: This man is extremely dangerous. His
    insidiously inflammatory message is particularly
    dangerous to young people who haven't been
    taught to ignore him yet. He changes men and
    claims to set them free.
WARNING: HE IS STILL AT LARGE!

From "Is God dead?" to "Jesus is still at large!" It shows just how much things had changed in such a short period of time. In Southern California, a pastor named Chuck Smith opened the church up to young hippie kids to come in off the beach and hear the gospel, and soon his church was overflowing.

Other churches overflowed also as the Jesus Movement spread around the globe. Thousands of churches have been impacted by what God did during this time. For all practical purposes, contemporary Christian music and contemporary praise and worship was born during the Jesus Movement.

But guess what?

That was more than forty years ago, and many of those young hippie kids are grandparents now. (I should know. I'm one of them. And I came to faith during the Jesus Movement.)

The church where I pastor, Harvest Christian Fellowship, and the evangelistic Harvest Crusades grew directly out of the Jesus Movement. We have seen more than four million people in attendance around the world at those crusades, and some 400,000 people have made commitments to follow Christ.

But we need another Jesus Movement. We need

another Great Awakening. We need to start praying for a spiritual awakening in our country.

REVIVAL: EMOTION OR DIVINE INVASION?

If God visits America again, it probably won't look like past revivals. It likely won't look like the Great Awakenings of the eighteenth and nineteenth centuries or the Jesus Movement of the twentieth century. We really don't know what it would look like. It isn't something we can predetermine; it isn't something we can organize. It's something for which we must agonize in prayer. We say, "Lord, send it! We need Your sovereign touch on our nation again."

We know for certain that at some point, revival will come to our world. In Revelation 7, we read of a multitude of believers so large that they can't be numbered in heaven. These are people who will be saved in the Tribulation period, when the Antichrist is ruling. I don't expect to be around for that time. I believe that if you have placed your faith in Christ, you will be caught up to meet the Lord in the air before the Antichrist is revealed and the Tribulation period begins (see

1 Thessalonians 4:13-18). Nevertheless, we read of millions of people who come to faith during this time of unprecedented international crisis.

Christians like to use the word *revival* quite a bit. But what do we really mean by it? Richard Owens Roberts described it like this: "the extraordinary movement of the Holy Spirit producing extraordinary results." Another said, "Revival is a community saturated with God." A. W. Tozer defined revival as that which changes the moral climate of a community. Revival is *not* an emotion or people working themselves into a state of excitement; revival is an invasion from heaven that brings people to an awareness of God and their need for Him and His intervention.

Actually, revival is a church word, and it is meant for believers. Nonbelievers don't need revival; they need evangelism. That is why we are to go into all of the world and preach the gospel. It is Christians who need revival, and if we are revived, I believe we also will evangelize.

It is my belief that most Americans have not heard the authentic gospel message. Many Americans have heard preaching—perhaps snatches of Christian messages from radio or TV—and have developed some pretty strange ideas about God. But I wonder how many have really heard the authentic gospel.

I don't think our country is populated with outright atheists or pagans as much as it is filled with a group of "almost Christians." Who are "almost Christians"? They have heard enough about Jesus and the gospel to confuse them but not enough to save them. In Acts 26:28, King Agrippa said to the apostle Paul, "You almost persuade me to become a Christian"—in other words, "Almost, but not quite."

I believe that many Americans fall into that category of "almost but not quite" believers. We like the word *almost*. It's a handy word, isn't it? If you are late for a meeting, someone from the office might ring your cell phone and say, "Where are you? The meeting is starting." And you might reply, "Oh. . . . Um, I'm *almost* there." What does that mean? It could mean, "I just rolled out of bed."

Or maybe if you're going out to dinner with your wife and she's taking a little bit longer to get ready than you had anticipated, you say to her, "Honey, the reservation is in ten minutes. Are you ready yet?"

And she might reply, "Almost!" (That is woman-speak for another hour, minimum.)

In the same sense, there are multitudes of "almost Christians." The trouble is that you can't be an "almost Christian." It's like being pregnant: You are or you aren't.

Statistics will show that most Americans believe in God, believe in heaven, and say that Jesus is the Son of God and rose from the dead.

That sounds good.

At the same time, however, half of all Americans who consider themselves Christians don't believe that Satan exists, one-third believe that Jesus sinned while He was on earth, and a quarter of those "believers" dismiss the idea that the Bible is accurate in all it teaches.

How do those numbers fit together? They *don't*. So what we have in our country is a great deal of uncertainty and misunderstanding.

When we look at the complex and often heartbreaking problems in our nation today, we might be inclined to blame a particular politician or political party or philosophy. We point our fingers and say, "He is our problem" or "She is our problem." But I want you to notice where God points His finger when a nation breaks down spiritually and morally.

"IF MY PEOPLE . . ."

> If My people who are called by My name will humble themselves, and pray and seek My face, and turn from their wicked ways, then I will hear from heaven, and will forgive their sin and heal their land.
> (2 Chronicles 7:14)

In the context of biblical history, this statement was given to Israel at the dedication of the first temple in Jerusalem. King Solomon was there, at the height of his power, and Israel was enjoying an unprecedented era of prosperity and God's blessing.

But the Lord knew their hearts. He knew that this flurry of excitement over worshipping Him wouldn't last. In verse 14, He was saying, "When you turn away from Me in future days and life begins to fall apart for you, I want you to remember these things. Humble yourselves. Pray. Seek My face. Turn from your wicked ways. And I will hear you and heal you."

What was true for Israel is true for the United States in the twenty-first century as well, as a nation that was built on a Judeo-Christian foundation.

Notice that the last part of this verse is a promise: "Then I will hear from heaven, and will forgive their sin and heal their land." This is what we want to see! We want to see America healed. We want to see our nation forgiven and restored to fellowship with God.

So what does God say? "If My people who are called by My name will humble themselves, and pray and seek My face, and turn from their wicked ways . . ."

Again, it is easy to identify our country's "wicked ways" with certain people or groups. It's the Democrats' fault. It's the Republicans' fault. It's Hollywood's fault. It's Congress. It's the White House. It's the unions. It's the media. It's the Tea Party.

But God says, "Listen people, the problem is in *My* house, with *My* people. If My people would live as they ought to live and pray as they ought to pray, it would impact a nation. But because My people are not behaving as they ought to, the nation is breaking down. My people need to humble themselves and pray."

That is why revival must begin with the church, but more on that in the next chapter.

Pray and seek His face.

The word used here for *pray* is interesting. Of the twelve Hebrew words employed to express the single verb "to pray," the one used here could be translated "to judge self habitually."

What a revelation, when you think about the times in which we are living. We live in a culture almost completely absorbed with *self*. We have been told for years that the reason people do bad things is because "they lack self-esteem" and that we all need "more self-love." Further, if each of us had a better self-image, everything would be so much better.

Is that true?

No, it isn't.

God says that what you and I need to do is judge ourselves habitually. In other words, it means we need to recognize that we have evil hearts and we live out our years on earth with evil tendencies.

Sometimes you will hear Christians say, "Well, God knows my heart, so who are you to judge me?"

Yes, God truly does know our hearts. And guess what? They are wicked. So we need to quit rationalizing bad behavior and judge ourselves habitually.

Malcolm Muggeridge once said, "Where, then, does happiness lie? In forgetfulness, not indulgence, of the self. In escape from sensual appetites, not in their satisfaction."[3] In fact, the Bible identifies self-love as one of the primary sins of the last days. In 2 Timothy 3:1-2, we are told, "There will be terrible times in the last days. People will be lovers of themselves" (NIV). Or as the Phillips translation puts it, "Men will become utterly self-centered."

So what does it mean to "judge self habitually"? It means to do a little spiritual evaluation every day and ask yourself questions such as these: *Am I where I ought to be spiritually? Should I be growing more? Should I be learning more? Am I the man or woman of God that I ought to be, or is there room for improvement?*

Of course there is room for improvement! The moment you think you have "arrived," it only proves you aren't even close. After years of walking with the Lord, the apostle Paul said, "I do not consider myself to have 'arrived,' spiritually, nor do I consider myself already perfect. But I keep going on, grasping ever more firmly that purpose for which Christ grasped me" (Philippians 3:12, PH).

David prayed like this: "Search me, O God, and know my heart; test my thoughts. Point out anything you find in me that makes you sad, and lead me along the path of everlasting life" (Psalm 139:23-24, TLB).

It has been said that self-satisfaction is the death of progress. We need to judge ourselves, asking ourselves where we are in life and where we ought to be. And if we're not where we ought to be, we need to make the necessary changes and pray to God for His enabling, forgiveness, and restoring touch on both ourselves and our nation.

One historian pointed out that there has never been such a thing in history as a prayer-less revival. We need to pray and seek His face.

What does "seek His face" mean? The Hebrew word for seek means "to search out" or "strive after." Have you ever lost your wallet, your purse, or maybe a new iPhone? It's a terrible feeling. You turn everything upside down looking for it, or you try to retrace your steps, racking your brain trying to remember when you had it last.

Seeking God, then, speaks of an earnestness and consistency in prayer. You are very, very serious about it and intent on the task. Much of our prayer has no power in it because there is no heart in it. And if we put so little heart into our prayers, we can't expect God to put much heart into answering them. We need to pray, pouring out our hearts to God for our country. When was the last time you did that?

Turn from sinful ways.

As Scripture says, we need to turn from our wicked ways. Remember, this is addressed to *believers*. Many of us like to point our fingers at this national sin or that godless tendency in our country; but what God is talking about here is the personal sin of His own people! God is saying, "My people need to turn from their wicked ways."

The fact is that all of the prayer in the world isn't going to make any difference if you have unconfessed sin in your life. The psalmist said, "If I regard iniquity in my heart, the Lord will not hear me" (Psalm 66:18,

KJV). The word used for "regard" there means "to hold on to" or "cling to." In Isaiah 59, we read these words:

Listen! The LORD's arm is not too weak to save you,
nor is his ear too deaf to hear you call.
It's your sins that have cut you off from God.
Because of your sins, he has turned away
and will not listen anymore. (verses 1-2, NLT)

Attempting to pray while you are living in known sin is like hanging up the phone to heaven. It's like trying to make a call on your cell when the battery is dead: You won't get through.

You may have a phone like my little granddaughters have, with a little electronic chip in it. It's called the Dora the Explorer phone. And if you push the button, you get Dora's voice and can have an imaginary conversation. The trouble is, Dora isn't really there; it's just a recording. You never really have a connection at all.

It's the same with trying to talk to God when you have known, unconfessed sin in your life. You can talk all you want, but there is no connection.

You say, "What do you mean 'sin in my life'? What

are you talking about?" For starters, we could talk about the sins of *commission* and the sins of *omission*. A sin of commission is doing what you know you shouldn't do, but the sin of omission is *not* doing what you know you *should* do. Maybe the Lord has put it on your heart to pray more, share the gospel with a neighbor, or contribute financially to the work of the kingdom of God.

If you know that God is speaking to you about one or more of these things and you close your ears and your heart to what He is saying, that can be a sin of omission. The Bible says, "Anyone, then, who knows the good he ought to do and doesn't do it, sins" (James 4:17, NIV). God is saying, "Turn from those sins. Turn from the deliberate sins and acts of evil in your life. Turn from ignoring My voice and the sin of refusing to do what you know you should do." Until you do turn from those things, praying isn't going to be of any help to you.

MAKING IT PERSONAL

Let's personalize this for a moment. Let's look again at 2 Chronicles 7:14, inserting our own name in place of the words *My people.* For me, it would look like this: "If Greg Laurie will humble himself and pray and seek My face and turn from his wicked ways, I will hear from heaven and will forgive Greg's sin."

Revival, you see, is personal. Don't just think about the church as a whole; think about yourself as an individual. So instead of talking about the church's needing revival, ask yourself, *Do I need revival? Do I need to get back to where I once was in my walk with God?*

Charles Finney gave one of the best definitions of revival I have read: "the renewal of the first love of Christians resulting in the awakening and conversion of sinners to God." Now, where have we heard that phrase "first love" in speaking of Christians before? In fact, Jesus Himself coined that phrase in Revelation 2, in a letter to the church at Ephesus. First, He commended them for the things they were doing right:

> I know your deeds, your hard work and your persever-
> ance. I know that you cannot tolerate wicked men,
> that you have tested those who claim to be apostles
> but are not, and have found them false. You have

persevered and have endured hardships for my name,
and have not grown weary. (verses 2-3, NIV)

In many ways, this was an admirable church. It was
a solidly grounded, hardworking, discerning, faithful
church. They even had remained loyal to Christ in the
face of hardships and persecution.

Yet in spite of this impressive track record, there
was a problem with these believers. Jesus continued and
said, "Yet I hold this against you: You have forsaken
your first love. Remember the height from which you
have fallen! Repent and do the things you did at first. If
you do not repent, I will come to you and remove your
lampstand from its place" (verses 4-5, NIV). Jesus was
saying, "You don't love Me as you did at first." This is a
form of what we sometimes call backsliding. When we
think of a backslider, we normally think of someone
like the prodigal son, running away from home and
living in debauchery and immorality. That is backsliding for sure. But a backslider is also someone who
has simply stopped *moving forward* in Christ.

Here is the hard truth: You are either moving forward as a believer in Christ or going backward. There

is no standing still. You can't hover in one place like a helicopter. And the sad fact is that it's often the little things that bring a believer down, not the big, dramatic sins.

It's a proven fact that termites destroy more structures each year than fires do. Unnoticed and undiscovered, these little antlike creatures eat away at the fibers of your home. No, they don't make headlines or the evening news, like a house fire might, but termites destroy more homes than all fires in America put together.

People's turning away from Christ is like a bunch of little termites slowly eating away at the walls and floorboards. What do the "termites" look like? Maybe a little compromise here, a little rationalization there, a gradual lowering of personal standards, and an increasing tendency to choose comfort or pleasure or self-protection at the expense of wholehearted obedience and a daily walk with God.

REDISCOVER YOUR FIRST LOVE

Jesus said to the believers in Ephesus, "You have left your first love" (Revelation 2:4). Notice He didn't say you have *lost* your first love. The good news is that it still can be found.

When I lose something (which is pretty much every day), I have to retrace my steps. A little earlier, I mentioned losing a cell phone. That's a big problem for me. I'm always taking it out and setting it down somewhere. So how do I find it after I've misplaced it? I call my own number and listen for the ring! (And hope that it isn't on mute.) If I dropped it in the car at night, I will call the number on someone else's cell phone and look for that little light—that little bit of luminescence in the dark. "Oh, great! There it is!" So I have to take the time to search for it and find it again.

We can do the same with our first love. *Go back to where you were before. Do the things you used to do.* In the words of Paul (McCartney, not the apostle), we need to get back, get back, get back to where we once belonged. So God promises that if we will pray, turn from our sinful ways, and humble ourselves, He will heal us.

This applies to an individual believer, to a broken family, to a church, and to a nation. God wants to send revival. He does! It's not as though He is saying, "I really don't want to do this, but if you talk Me into it, I might." No, the fact is that He wants to bless you even more than you want to be blessed. But you have a part in that. He wants you to participate in the process. He asks you to turn from your wicked ways, humble yourself, seek His face, and pray.

And if you do, He will hear from heaven.

That is a promise of God.

So whether we are talking about America as a nation or you and me as individual believers, we have a choice: revival or a closed heaven, spiritual awakening or judgment. Remember, however, that when God judges, He always starts with His own. As the apostle Peter said, judgment begins at the house of God (see 1 Peter 4:17).

And that's where revival starts too.

May it start with you, and may it start with me.

CHAPTER 3

I believe that the hope for America is the church.

"Wait," someone will say. "Didn't you say that the hope for America is a revival? Isn't it really God?

Exactly. The hope for America is God, working through His church.

What is revival? As we have said, it is Christians getting back to what they should have always been in the first place. It is Christians *coming back to life.* As we saw in the previous chapter, in 2 Chronicles 7:14 God promised that if His people would humble themselves, pray, seek His face, and turn from their sinful ways, He would hear from heaven, forgive their sin, and heal their nation.

We want to see our land healed.

We want to see America restored to a God-loving, God-fearing nation.

And God says that it starts with "My people."

Christians need to live up to their name by being Christ followers and by being Christlike. And if the church would be what it was meant to be, it would change our country.

But let's localize it. If *your* church would be what it ought to be, then it could change the city or town where you live. Let's now take it one step further. If *you* would be who and what *you* ought to be as a follower of Jesus and as a part of the church, then it could make a difference in your family, your home, your church, and your country.

FIRST IMPRESSIONS OF CHURCH

The first recollection I have of church was as a little boy with my grandparents. I didn't like it at all. I thought it was boring. And my grandmother kept shushing me. I remember drawing cartoons on the church bulletin as the preacher droned on and on.

When I was in military school for a few years, we went to a mandatory chapel. I didn't really enjoy that, either, but we had to go. I remember they would give us ten cents to put in the offering. The reason I remember that is because one Sunday I kept the ten cents and didn't give it to God.

I took that dime that was supposed to go in the offering plate and spent it at the canteen instead—the little store where they sold candy, school supplies, and such. I already had ten cents, but now I had twenty cents, which bought twice as much grape licorice (my favorite at the time). Bottom line, I really didn't have a lot to do with the church during my childhood. It wasn't something I was a part of or knew very much about.

I came to Christ at age seventeen on my high school campus. There was one very persistent guy named Mark who sort of appointed himself to be my friend. In what seemed like just hours after I received Christ, Mark came up to me and said, "Hey, Greg, I saw that you became a Christian. That's great! I want to take you to church."

"That's okay," I said. "I really don't want to go to church."

But Mark would have none of it. "No, no," he said. "You're going to church with me. Where do you live? I'll come pick you up." He was very insistent, in a friendly sort of way.

Finally I said, "All right. Fine." (I knew I probably wouldn't like it but that it wouldn't kill me.)

So Mark picked me up at my house and took me to church, and I had absolutely no idea what to expect. I think it was a Monday night or a Wednesday night at Calvary Chapel in Costa Mesa, California, right in the heyday of the Jesus Movement. The place was jammed with young people.

Whatever I might have been expecting, this wasn't it. There was something like electricity in the air, and it scared me a little. I thought, *I don't want to go into that place.* There was just too much happiness in there, too much smiling and hugging and loving. I didn't know how to handle it.

You have to understand that I was raised in a very dysfunctional home. The phrase "I love you" was never spoken in my home, and we didn't hug in our family.

But there was *a lot* of hugging going on that night, and I thought to myself, *Oh no, I don't want to be hugged.* I was walking carefully and cautiously, not knowing what I was getting into. Then some random girl came up to me with a big smile on her face and said, "God bless you, brother!" Then she threw her arms around me.

Oh, well. I guess I couldn't avoid it.

However, when I looked inside the auditorium and saw that the place was completely full, I felt a little surge of relief. I thought, *There's no way we can get a seat in here. Now I can go home.*

"Well, Mark," I said over the hubbub, "there's no room in here."

"Yeah," he said, disappointed. "I wish we could get a seat."

At that moment (wouldn't you know it?), someone in the front row recognized me from the high school Bible study and waved us over. So I walked through the crowd, certain that everyone was looking at me. I felt terribly self-conscious as I squeezed into a seat in the front row. But what I didn't realize at the time was that I had a front-row seat to a genuine revival.

So I sat there, waiting for the service to begin, wondering what would happen next. Then the music started. Back in the days of the Jesus Movement, people in church would sometimes put their arms around each other and sway back and forth to the music. So people on both sides of me put their arms around me, and the whole row started swaying. There was no escaping it!

I thought, *I don't want these arms around me. I don't want to be here. I don't want to sway.* They were all singing, "Love, love, love, love."

Christians! What had I gotten into?

When the song was over, everyone pointed straight up at the ceiling with their index fingers. That was the big symbol back in those days: the "one way" sign, meaning one way to God, through Jesus. So everybody was pointing up, and I had no idea what was happening. What was I supposed to do—see something on the ceiling?

After the singing, the preacher came out, a middle-aged bald guy named Chuck Smith. That was about the last thing I wanted to see. He looked like a high school teacher—or worse, a principal. *Oh no*, I said to myself, *this is going to be so boring!*

Then he opened up the Word of God and I forgot about everything else. Wonder of wonders, it made sense to me—to *me*, a brand-new believer. It was relevant to me. And the fear in my heart began to melt away. In fact, I went from being uncomfortable in church to where you couldn't get me out of the church. I went to every service possible at Calvary Chapel of Costa Mesa, and I wanted to be a part of everything and learn as much as I could learn. Just two years later, I went to Riverside, planting a church myself.

It wasn't that I understood I was planting a church at the time. I thought I was just teaching a Bible study for young people at a local Episcopal church. But it began to grow and grow. Pretty soon, people were calling me "pastor." I would think, *Me? No . . . I can't be your pastor.*

I tried to find someone to take over the Bible study, but I couldn't. It finally dawned on me that the Lord was truly calling me to be a pastor in that place.

Fast-forward forty years or so, and now I'm the old bald guy teaching from God's Word. Ironic, isn't it? But let me say this: I am as committed to the mission of the church as I was on the day when I first discovered how wonderful church can be.

WHAT IS A CHURCH, ANYWAY?

You might be surprised to learn that the first person to use that word wasn't Paul or any of the other apostles. It was Jesus Himself:

> When Jesus came into the region of Caesarea Philippi, He asked His disciples, saying, "Who do men say that I, the Son of Man, am?"
>
> So they said, "Some say John the Baptist, some Elijah, and others Jeremiah or one of the prophets."
>
> He said to them, "But who do you say that I am?"
>
> Simon Peter answered and said, "You are the Christ, the Son of the living God."
>
> Jesus answered and said to him, "Blessed are you, Simon Bar-Jonah, for flesh and blood has not revealed this to you, but My Father who is in heaven. And I also say to you that you are Peter, and *on this rock I will build My church, and the gates of Hades shall not prevail against it.*" (Matthew 16:13-18, emphasis added)

When Jesus walked this earth, He started only one organization: His church. By stating that the gates of hell would not prevail against it, Jesus was saying, "Listen, the church is here to stay. It will prevail against all odds and be My witness until I call it home."

What does the word *church* mean? It comes from the Greek word *ecclesia*, which is made up of two other Greek words. One of those terms is *out from* and the other word is *called*.

Called out from.

Called out from what? Called out from this world. Called out from this culture. Jesus is saying, "My followers should be separate from this culture." We not only are called out from, we are "called together to." We are called to God, and we are called to each other.

Maybe you have attended one of our Harvest Crusades at Angel Stadium in Anaheim, California. It's an amazing experience when thousands of Christians gather in that place.

Over the years, I've been to Angel Stadium for a number of other events too. I've seen U2 and Paul McCartney in concert there, and the staging was incredible. I've been to Angels games there as well. But it's a funny thing: When God's people gather together in Angel Stadium, it turns into a sanctuary. Why? Because the church is not a building; it is people. And Jesus said, "Where two or three are gathered together in My name, I am there in the midst of them" (Matthew 18:20).

That's what the church is: God's people with Jesus in their midst.

Jesus made His "On this rock I will build My church" statement at a place called Caesarea Philippi, which happened to be a center of paganism and false belief. In fact, Caesarea Philippi was named after the Greek god Pan. If you go to Caesarea Philippi today, you can see what is left of a site dedicated to idols and false gods. So here in this place of false worship, Jesus asked His disciples to make a statement and a stand.

In this place of paganism, Christ asked them a probing question: "Who do men say that I am?" (see 16:13).

It's impressive to make your stand for Christ among fellow Christians who know you and love you. But it's even more impressive when you make your stand for Christ out in the culture, where there are people who neither know nor love Jesus. It's one thing to declare your love for Jesus on a Sunday morning at church or in a Wednesday night Bible study or with several of your Christian friends, but it's a different thing altogether to make that declaration on Monday morning at work, in the classroom, or in your neighborhood.

The Lord was basically saying, "Okay, guys, as you get out and about, rubbing shoulders with people, what are they saying about Me? What's the word on the street?"

"Some say John the Baptist, some Elijah, and others Jeremiah or one of the prophets," the answer came (verse 14).

"But who do you say that I am?" (verse 15).

Inspired by the Holy Spirit, Simon Peter immediately piped up and said, "You are the Christ, the Son of the living God" (verse 16).

Jesus looked at him and replied, "Flesh and blood has not revealed this to you, but My Father who is in heaven" (verse 17).

Can you imagine how Peter felt at that moment? Don't forget that these disciples were always competing with each other, arguing about who would get the best seat and who was going to be top dog in the kingdom of heaven. And then Jesus said *this* to Peter? In the old King James language, the words kind of roll off the tongue: "Bless art thou, Simon Barjona" (verse 17).

Can you visualize him in that moment? I wonder if he kind of puffed out his chest a little and maybe glanced sideways at James and John.

But what is Jesus saying here? That He would build His church on Simon Peter? No, of course not. He was saying the church would be built on what Peter had just declared, under the inspiration of God, the Holy Spirit. What did Peter say? "You are the Christ, the Son of the living God." The foundation of the church is Christ Himself.

He went on to say that the gates of hell would not prevail against it. This reminds us that the church always will face hostility and opposition, and so it has through the millennia.

But this isn't saying that the church would be under attack as much as it is saying that the church would advance in the face of opposition. Gates, as in "the gates of hell," don't attack. Gates are part of a fortress that seeks to defend. And as the church seeks to advance the kingdom and pull men and women from the clutches of Satan, the Devil will say, "You guys back off! Don't you be treading on my turf!"

But Jesus was saying, "No, the church will prevail."

Yes, we may lose a battle here and there. As in any war, there will be casualties. Martyrs will have to shed their blood and give up their lives, just as it has been since the days of Stephen.

But never doubt this: We will win the war!

I have read the last page of the Bible, and I know that we win in the end. We can't allow ourselves to become discouraged or overwhelmed by the battles we face, which can be intense. We can't be deterred. We must press forward.

JESUS LOVES THE CHURCH

Sometimes you will hear Christians say, "I love the Lord—I just don't love the church." But that really isn't an option. First John 5:1 says, "Everyone who believes that Jesus is the Christ has become a child of God. And everyone who loves the Father loves his children, too" (NLT).

When I become friends with someone—and I

have many friends whom I've known for twenty-five to thirty years—I become friends with their kids, too. If I love someone as a friend, my love naturally extends to their family, and their kids become like nieces and nephews to me. In the same way, when we love God, we also will love His children. And if you don't love His children, one has to question how much you really love God. It's somewhat fashionable these days to talk down to (or "dis") the church. But understand this: When you are cynical or dismissive about the church, you are speaking critically of someone whom Jesus loves.

I don't know about you, but the best way to really offend me is to insult my wife. People walk up to me all the time and say, "Greg, I disagree with this and I disagree with that."

And I will reply, "Okay. Let's talk about that."

But it's a different matter altogether if you make a disparaging remark about my wife. If you talk smack about my wife, I might want to smack you! Say what you like about me, but don't speak a word against her. I take that very personally.

So who is the church? We are the bride of Christ. We belong to Him, and He loves us. Paul uses that marriage analogy very clearly in Ephesians 5:25, where we read, "Husbands, this means love your wives, just as Christ loved the church. He gave up his life for her" (NLT).

Some people claim to be Christians yet don't attend church. But if you really are a Christian, longing to be with God's people just goes with the territory.

You might say, "I haven't found a church that I like yet. I just watch different services on the Internet." But listen to what the Bible says in Hebrews 10:24-25: "Let us think of ways to motivate one another to acts of love and good works. And let us not neglect our meeting together, as some people do, but encourage one another, especially now that the day of his return is drawing near" (NLT).

Note that this verse does not say, "Let us not neglect our meeting together . . . unless, of course, Sunday is your only day off. Or you have a triathlon you want to compete in. Or it's a great beach day—then you are excused, because you don't really need fellowship as much as other Christians do."

No, if you love God, then you will love His people. If you love and respect Christ, then you will love and respect His chosen bride.

But what if you don't love God's people? What if you don't love and respect the bride of Christ? Are you really a Christian? The Bible makes this strong statement:

> If someone says, "I love God," but hates a Christian brother or sister, that person is a liar; for if we don't love people we can see, how can we love God, whom we cannot see? And he has given us this command: Those who love God must also love their Christian brothers and sisters. (1 John 4:20-21, NLT)

In other words, your desire for fellowship is like a barometer reading of your love for God. The more you love God, the more you will love to be in the church — a part of the church, loving the church. The less you love God, the less you will want to be around other Christians.

To those who say that the church is full of hypocrites, I say, "Come on in! There's always room for one more!"

No, I'm not excusing hypocrisy. But you will find

it—along with a host of other weaknesses and frail-
ties—wherever you find a group of imperfect people.
The church has its flaws because it is made up of people
like you and me.

Even so, Jesus started the church, died for the
church, loves the church, and someday will return to
earth for the church, taking her to heaven as His bride.

OUR NEED FOR FELLOWSHIP

A lack of desire for fellowship with other believers is a
good indication that an individual is starting to
backslide.

You say, "Hold it, Greg. That's a provocative
statement."

Maybe so, but I believe it to be true.

As I mentioned earlier, either we are moving forward in the Christian life or we are slipping backward.
It is progression or regression, and standing still is not
an option. So if you find yourself withdrawing from
church or backing off from your study of the Word of
God or giving up on your prayer life, you are starting
to backslide, whether you want to admit it or not. You

may not be in overt sin yet, but you are already setting the stage for it.

Backsliding always begins with relaxing your grip on that which you need before taking hold of that which will eventually destroy you. When you say, "I'm just too busy for church," that to me is an indication of spiritual sickness, like the beginnings of a fever.

How important is it to you that you are setting an example for your children and grandchildren? A study revealed that when Dad and Mom attend church regularly, 72 percent of their children will remain faithful in attendance. If only dad attends regularly, 55 percent of the children will remain faithful. If only mom attends regularly, 15 percent will remain faithful. If neither attends regularly, only 6 percent will remain faithful.

Do you see how it trickles down? You are setting an example that will have a powerful effect on your children's lifelong attitudes toward the church.

When you say, "We don't need to go today. I want to get in a round of golf," that decision will have a lasting impact.

Or maybe you say, "Let's not go today. I think it

might be raining and the roads could be dangerous," that is conveying a message that says, "This really isn't important to me. I can take it or leave it." Don't fool yourself; your kids *will* absorb that attitude, and it might continue to affect them, even after you have left this earth.

I've read articles that state that going to church is actually good for your health. Among other things, of people who undergo heart surgery, those who draw comfort from their faith and their church have a higher rate of survival than those who don't. The blood pressure of people who attend church is noticeably lower than those who don't. People with faith who attend church regularly experience less depression than people who don't. And suicide is four times higher among non-churchgoers than churchgoers.

Those may be interesting fringe benefits, but the real reason we should come together in worship is because God works in unique and powerful ways when His people gather together in His name. It is in church that we refocus, learn, and grow. It is where most of us first came to Christ and, in many cases, where we bring others to faith in Him. And it is here that we help one

another discover, use, and develop the spiritual gifts
God has given to each one of us.

WHY DOES THE CHURCH EXIST?

The church exists to glorify God, edify (or build up)
the saints, and evangelize the world. That's one way to
remember it. A simpler way might say the church's
mission is *upward*, *inward*, and *outward*.

1. We are here to glorify God. (That's upward.)

The church is here to glorify and honor God, and (by
the way) so are you. Apart from the church, your own
purpose for being on earth is to bring God glory. The
Bible says that He has created all things for His pleasure. In Ephesians 1:12, we are told that we are to be
for "the praise of His glory."

That is why we worship the Lord in song.
Worship is essentially prayer set to music. This is
why you never should be late to church, missing the
worship but getting there in time for the message.
What you miss out on is the time when God is glori-
fied. The Bible tells us that He inhabits the praises of

His people (see Psalm 22:3, kjv).

In other words, worship isn't a warm-up act for the message. No, the hymns and worship songs are to help prepare our hearts to receive the Word of God.

When we engage in worship, it is a powerful witness. How so? I believe that when a nonbeliever comes into a setting where Christians are honestly encountering God, it is a testimony to him or her because there is nothing in the world like it.

People in our country rarely sing together anymore. There was a time in our history when Americans would sing songs together, just for fun, perhaps around the piano. But you rarely see that these days. In fact, very few people even will attempt to sing along with the national anthem at sporting events.

True, some sing well and others can hardly carry a tune, but that really doesn't matter or enter into it. Christians sing from happy hearts. It is the overflow of joy coming from a people who have been saved, redeemed, and brought up close to the heart of God. And that kind of singing makes an impression on nonbelievers.

Christian music was one of the things that drew

me to the little Bible study on my high school campus
where I ended up coming to Christ. And the fact that
there was a cute girl there I wanted to meet didn't hurt
either. Nevertheless, when I spotted her on the front
lawn of our campus with her Christian friend, I sat
down too, and my first impression was being amazed
at their music. Back then, of course, the music was
really simple and unsophisticated. There were simple
little choruses they sang over and over again, with just
a few chords on a guitar.

Up until that point, I had considered myself a real
music connoisseur: I was into the Beatles, Led
Zeppelin, Jimi Hendrix, and the Doors. But when I
listened to those simple songs and saw that those kids
were completely into it and singing with all their
hearts, it moved me deeply. It wasn't because they were
good singers or musicians; it was because these people
were actually encountering God, and I had never seen
anything like it.

If you are engaged in worship, encountering God
and just soaking in His presence and His nearness, I
think that nonbelievers look over at you and say to
themselves, *Wow. I don't have that kind of relationship*

with God. This might be real. By the same token, however, if they look over at you while you are texting a
friend, surfing the Internet, or talking to someone
during worship, they may conclude there is really
nothing to it.

It is also a powerful testimony when a Christian
can rejoice in the Lord even when going through grief
or suffering or great hardship.

In Acts 16, we read about Paul and Silas, who were
savagely beaten and thrown into a dungeon for preaching the gospel in Philippi. Even though they were
bruised and bloodied and chained up like animals,
they were praying and singing hymns in that dreadful
place. And, according to verse 25, the other prisoners
were listening! The word used in Scripture for "listening" means "to listen with pleasure."

It was music to their ears. Why? Was it because
these guys harmonized so well and knew some catchy
songs? No, it was because the other prisoners had
never heard anything like it before, and it stunned
them to think that these two Christians could sing
and praise God after what they had just suffered and
were suffering.

Asaph the psalmist was grappling with the age-old question of "Why do the wicked prosper?" After struggling with that for a while and working himself into a depression, something dawned on him in Psalm 73:16-17: "When I tried to understand all this, it was oppressive to me till I entered the sanctuary of God; then I understood their final destiny" (NIV).

Asaph essentially was saying, "I didn't understand why things are the way that they are until I came into God's presence, to study His Word with His people. Then I saw things in proper perspective."

You can come to church with big problems, and when you walk out the doors, your problems are still there. But it is then that you see them the right way! You might have walked in thinking, *Big problems, small God*, but you walk out remembering, *Big God, small problems.*

On the Thursday the Lord called our son Christopher home, we experienced the worst day of our entire lives. We were completely devastated. But when Sunday came around, I knew there was only one place I wanted to be: at church.

People were amazed by that. But why would they

be amazed? Church is the best place for hurting people. Church is a place that gives us help and focus and where we receive God's Word. And if I ever had needed those things, I needed them right then. So I came in my grief and sorrow, and I worshipped the Lord. God gave me perspective that day, and He helped me.

I really can't imagine withdrawing from church and God's people after something bad happens. Those are times we need to *run to* the church and find that encouragement that fellow believers can provide.

2. We are here to edify other believers. (That's inward.)

The apostle Paul said that his goal was to warn believers and teach them with all the wisdom God had given him.

As pastor at Harvest Christian Fellowship, I fully understand that my opinions are no more valuable than anyone else's. People don't come to hear my opinions (or my jokes); they come to hear the careful and consistent teaching of the Word of God.

You show me a church where this isn't happening, and I have to wonder, *What's the point?* Little fifteen-minute topical talks are okay in their place, but what people really need every week is solid teaching, straight from the pages of the Bible. I've heard it said that sermonettes produce Christianettes, and I tend to agree. We need God's Word. Otherwise, why do we bother?

Hebrews 4:12 says, "The word of God is alive and powerful. It is sharper than the sharpest two-edged sword, cutting between soul and spirit, between joint and marrow. It exposes our innermost thoughts and desires" (NLT). Martin Luther said, "The Bible is alive, it speaks to me; it has feet, it runs after me; it has hands, it lays hold of me."[1]

When we read about the church of the first century—the church in revival, the church that changed its world—we read that "they continued steadfastly in the apostles' doctrine and fellowship, in the breaking of bread, and in prayers" (Acts 2:42).

The phrase *continued steadfastly* speaks of real passion. They were living in a first-love relationship with Jesus Christ, and they applied themselves to what was being taught from the Word.

As we long for and pray for revival in our nation in these days, I think we need more than anointed preaching and teaching; I think we also need anointed listening. What does that mean? That means . . .

I come to church with my Bible.

It's a trend in some churches for people to leave their Bibles at home. All of the Bible verses are up on the screen behind the pastor or there are Bibles in the pew that you can borrow. I think it's better for us to bring our own Bibles, open our own Bibles, and read out of our own Bibles. It helps us remember that the authority doesn't lie with the pastor; rather, it rests in the pages of the Word of God.

I come to church ready to listen with attention.

We listen with attention, and it is attention with intention. Take notes on what you hear. We should hunger for God's Word like a little baby desires milk. In fact, we are told in 1 Peter 2:2, "You must crave pure spiritual milk so that you will grow into a full experience of salvation. Cry out for this nourishment" (NLT).

One day when our son Christopher was a little boy, before he could speak, he went and stood in front of the refrigerator, just staring at it. He kept repeating the phrase, "Yom, yom!"

We thought, *There must be something in there that he wants.* So we opened it up and pulled out the eggs. No, that wasn't it.

"Yom, yom," he said. We took out a loaf of bread. That wasn't it either, and Christopher was getting insistent.

"Yom, YOM!" After going through a number of other items, I finally grabbed the milk. He reached for it and said, "Yom, yom." So we learned that milk is "yom, yom" in baby speak.

That is how we should hunger for the Word of God: Nothing else will do, and we will accept no substitutes!

Not only should you be a part of the church, you should attach yourself to one church and become an active part of it. Some churches have membership, and others don't. I won't argue either way here except to say that you need to plug into one church instead of playing the field and attending numerous churches at once.

Why? Because you need a pastor who can influence you and to whom you can be accountable.

Yes, there are a lot of great churches out there, and that is certainly true in Southern California, where I live and serve as a pastor. You could hop on the freeway on a Saturday night or Sunday morning and find yourself at one of many good Bible-teaching churches. But there is a problem with circulating among two or three churches at a time and not having a home base: You never get a chance to connect with the people or with the church leadership. We pastors are here to help you with your spiritual growth and watch over your soul, and the Bible tells us that we will be held accountable for how well we do that.

But how can we fulfill that task if you are with us only one out of four Sundays? How can we teach you a consistent theology if you are moving around so much that you don't know what to believe?

First Timothy 4:16 says, "Watch your life and doctrine closely. Persevere in them, because if you do, you will save both yourself and your hearers" (NIV). What you believe matters. In fact, it's critical. That is why I never have understood people's rating a church on what I consider to be peripheral issues, such as facilities or convenience or driving time to get there. If I weren't a pastor, the first thing I would be looking for is a church that teaches the Word of God. That is number one. It wouldn't matter to me if they had the greatest facility or if it were right next door to me—I want to go where I will be taught the Word of God.

People sometimes flit from church to church because they don't like this or they don't like that. But maybe the problem isn't with the church; maybe the problem is with you. Your perspective might change if you took time to put down some roots and become part of a congregation.

Comparing teachers with teachers and pastors with pastors happened in the early church, too. Paul wrote to the believers in Corinth,

> You are jealous of one another and quarrel with each other. Doesn't that prove you are controlled by your sinful nature? Aren't you living like people of the world? When one of you says, "I am a follower of Paul," and another says, "I follow Apollos," aren't you acting just like people of the world?
>
> After all, who is Apollos? Who is Paul? We are only God's servants through whom you believed the Good News. Each of us did the work the Lord gave us.
> (1 Corinthians 3:3-5, NLT)

Why should you have a home church? You need to have a place where you can regularly invest your finances and become personally engaged.

Sometimes I think we treat churches with a consumer mentality, similar to the way we would treat restaurants and movie theaters. We will say, "I went to that restaurant last week. Let's go to another one." But the church isn't a restaurant. The church is a family, and you need to be part of the family.

Maybe one of the reasons you feel as though you're not getting enough out of church is because you're not putting enough into it. You come intermittently and don't commit yourself. But maybe if you settled in and became a part of a local church, it would mean more to you because "you have skin in the game."

Stop thinking of the church as "them," and start thinking of the church as "us." Be a part of the family, take the gifts God has given you, and develop them and use them for His glory. I suggest that your church experience could completely change for you if you stopped coming as a spectator and instead joined the team.

3. We are here to evangelize the world. (That's outward.)

We become part of a church to glorify God, to edify and build up one another, and, finally, to take the gospel to our region, our nation, and our world. I believe that this final part of our mission is a natural outgrowth of the first two.

In other words, if we are truly seeking to glorify God in our worship and we are building up one another in the faith, we will want to share the hope of salvation with others through our loving actions and words. Healthy sheep will reproduce themselves. Jesus has told us to go out into this culture as light — light in a darkened world.

How do we shine our light? Jesus said, "Let your light so shine before men, that they may see your good works and glorify your Father in heaven" (Matthew 5:16).

The church of Jesus Christ does that throughout America, in small towns and big cities alike. We feed people, clothe people, and help get people off drugs and alcohol. We counsel couples with messed-up marriages and parents having trouble with their kids. We help people in every way we can, and we do it in the name of Jesus. We are a light in this community that we call America.

But we are also called to be salt.

Jesus said in Matthew 5:13, "You are the salt of the earth. But if the salt loses its saltiness, how can it be made salty again? It is no longer good for anything" (NIV).

Salt in biblical times was used as a preservative, and we as Christians are a preservative in our culture. We stand up for what is right and true. We register and vote our conscience, informed by our biblical worldview, and we make no apology for that. As followers of Jesus, we are going to oppose sin.

The story is told of when President Calvin Coolidge returned home from church one Sunday and his wife asked him what the minister talked about. Coolidge, a man of few words, said, "Oh, he spoke on sin."

His wife said, "Well, yes. What else did he say?"

President Coolidge responded, "He was against it."

And so are we in the church of Jesus Christ. We are against sin. At the same time, however, we love sinners and want them to come to the Savior. That is why we are here. And God wants to use each one of us to touch our world and our community.

The only hope for the United States of America in what may be the world's final days is a revival that will sweep from sea to sea, waking up God's people and bringing tens of thousands of new believers into the kingdom of Christ.

Until that happens, we glorify God in worship, we build up our brothers and sisters in Christ, and we keep reaching out to our friends, family, neighbors, coworkers, and adversaries with the good news of salvation in Christ. Beyond that, we keep praying every day that God will visit our nation once again in great power and turn us back to Himself.

Revival begins with the church or it begins nowhere at all.

And the church is made up of individual believers.

In other words, revival begins with you.

NOTES

Chapter 1

1. "First Prayer of the Continental Congress, 1774," Office of the Chaplain, U.S. House of Representatives, http://chaplain.house.gov/archive/continental.html.
2. U.S. Congress, House, Congressional Record, 108th Congress, 1st sess., vol. 145—Part 15 (September 5, 2003), 21335.
3. U.S. Congress, House, Congressional Record, 21335.
4. Grant R. Jeffrey, *The Signature of God: Conclusive Proof That Every Teaching, Every Command, Every Promise in the Bible Is True* (Colorado Springs, CO: Waterbook, 2010), 26.
5. U.S. Congress, Senate, Congressional Record, 106th Congress, 2nd sess., vol. 146—Part 5 (May, 4, 2000), 6893.
6. C. H. Spurgeon, *The Sword and the Trowel* (London: Passmore and Alabaster, 1866), 529.
7. Spurgeon, 529.

Chapter 2

1. Will Durant, *Caesar and Christ* (New York: Simon & Schuster, 1944), 665.
2. William Joseph Federer, *America's God and Country: Encyclopedia of Quotations* (Saint Louis, MO: Amerisearch, Inc., 2000), 418.
3. Malcom Muggeridge, *Seeing Through the Eye: Malcom Muggeridge on Faith* (San Francisco: Ignatius, 2005), 39.

Chapter 3

1. Roy B. Zuck, *The Speaker's Quote Book: Over 5,000 Quotations and Illustrations for All Occasions* (Grand Rapids, MI: Kregel, 2009), 34.

Other Books by Greg Laurie

Visit www.kerygmapublishing.com